Going Back

Shelia Gaines

Parson's Porch Books

www.parsonsporchbooks.com

Going Back

ISBN: Softcover 978-1-951472-33-7

Copyright © 2020 by Shelia Gaines

All rights reserved. No part of this book may be reproduced or transmitted in any form or by any means, electronic or mechanical, including photocopying, recording, or by any information storage and retrieval system, without permission in writing from the publisher.

Going Back

Contents

Summertime in Shubuta When I was Young 7

Country Roads 9

Going Back 10

My Mama's Biscuits 11

Making groceries 12

in praise of good fathers everywhere… 13

Profound statements my daddy made 14

The Sound of Daddy's Voice 15

Old Writer 16

My Brother's Story as I Believe He Would Write It 18

Sugar Cane 20

Around the Bend in Bean Station 21

Snow Days 22

College 23

My Appalachian Heritage 24

Church Music 25

Lisa's Notes in the Sanctuary 26

Aunt Pearlie and the Cartwrights 27

Driving Lessons 28

Green Grass 29

Colloquial slang 30

How to Make a Crazy Quilt 31

The Woman and the Writer 32
Classically speaking as a Writer and a Librarian 33
stories I heard growing up that became my own 34
Rivers Continued... 36

Summertime in Shubuta When I was Young

I could burst open a watermelon
 and eat it right there in the field.
I could pull baby ears of corn from the stalk
 and watch my mama cut it from the cob.

Love ran down into that bowl right along with the milky
juices from the kernels.

I washed jars for jellies and pickles,
 peeled peaches, shucked corn, and shelled peas.
I would sit on the porch swing for hours
 in the shade of that big old pecan tree.

Cucumbers, tomatoes, strawberries and plums.

Lazy days for some;
Busy days for others.

My mama worked hardest on days she watched Daddy
 work tirelessly from sunup to sundown.
And when he worked his final sunset,
 she and my brothers worked on, though they tired.

There was a different revival
  at a different church every Sunday of the summer
months.
And some long-abandoned tradition required
  attending them all.

Revivals for salvation meant family, food and fellowship would abound.

I walked to softball games with my siblings
Some days we sat in hazy heat for hours.
Other days we ran home in the rain.

Lunch was supper and supper was dinner.
The one and only TV was always tuned to
Whatever Daddy wanted to watch
And we watched in awe!
Biscuits and syrup any time of the day or night
 was any meal that you wanted it to be.

I chose to forget some things...

I'll always remember summertime in Shubuta when I was young.

Country Roads

One county line blurs into another
Old church signs mark new sanctuaries
Hand-hewed rockers grace pristine porches
Lived-in homes look abandoned
Abandoned homes show signs of life
Open fields surround small houses
Locked gates lead to country mansions

Two car police force, fence rows, trestle bridges, cow pastures

Going Back

Where a gravel road
Dead-ends in Mudear's yard
Yonder is an everyday noun,
Reckon, an all-encompassing verb.
Across the corn field
Over the barbed-wire fence
Where an oak tree limb
Crashed through the roof
And rested in the middle
Of Aint P's living room
On top of the 10-year-old
Philco television.
Down the road behind the empty cow pasture
Where the family land
Runs all the way back
Before dirt roads were paved
Outhouses were brought in

Back before life was tweeted and posted
Before coffee was iced, mocha-ed and latte –ed
Water was caught in a rain barrel
Behind the house
Or pumped into a bucket
With a dipper that everyone drunk from

My Mama's Biscuits
(Ramblings about Love)

It's evident in all her cooking.
But more prevalent in the biscuits
Made with hands that
Can punctuate a statement
With the same intensity of a backhand lick,
Or softly pat a baby's burp.
She oversimplifies her biscuit making,
Mocking our insatiable appetite for them
She shares the recipe repeatedly
"Someone must learn this," she says
"Someone must carry the recipe on."
Her grandmother taught her to make biscuits
Way back when she was a child.
She made them in an iron skillet
Following grandmother's only mandate,
"You better not burn them biscuits!"
When my brother and his family drove from Atlanta
All the way to Shubuta, Mississippi just to taste a sample,
They went home with their stomachs full of love.

Making groceries

So why did you have to go "make groceries"?
The food was already made.
You just went to the store to buy it.
Maybe because you had to make your way to
Somewhere other than Shubuta to find a store.

in praise of good fathers everywhere...

The kids had gone off to swim that day
In June
Even the baby getting a chance to go
Because Daddy said she could

God in his infinite wisdom
Allowing her escape
From what would have been too painful to witness

Daddy worked hard in the summertime
Lived hard in the summertime
   ...Died in the summertime

Profound statements my daddy made

On my little sister
    Sometimes I can close my eyes and see her face
On false pretenses
    Anybody can put a big engine in a small car.
On how much money you needed
    Is he a big shot or a little shot?
On tight times
    You old enough to know I'm doing the best I can, right?
On television
    Ain't there a shoot 'em up on?
On tight jeans
    Did she have to grease herself to get in them pants?
On occasion when he could not find words
    Yes, yes, yes! (spoken with a negative shake of his head)

The Sound of Daddy's Voice

Part 1

>Daddy hollered so he could be heard
>That made his voice inaudible
>So, he just hollered louder

Part 2

>Daddy's lack of musical talent
>complemented his love to sing
>in a key unknown to any musician
>in a voice
>that held the ability to stir the souls
>of some of the hardest people...

Old Writer

The old writer smiles
        kindly at the young man who mocks
contemplation.
Laughs out loud,
        confidently challenges the youth to own the phrase
"Back in my day!"

The old writer respects
        women who wear hats and hose in hundred-
degree heat.
Looks back now,
        contrasts hand-held funeral parlor fans and single
air-conditioning units.

The old writer juxtaposes
        the beauty of ancient trees dripping Spanish moss
into the Chickasawhay River
Against the ugliness
        of decades old secrets surrounding a bridge
crossing it downstream.

The old writer knows
        the tangible taste of love in Mama's biscuits and
preserves.
Ventures back home for them
        over brick hard dirt roads cooked in the Mississippi
sun.

The old writer embraces
        the full history of the great Magnolia state.
Ponders from time to time,

      the literary and theatrical interpretations of racial inequity
Then and now…

The old writer remembers
      ice cold watermelon as vividly as elementary school racism.
Dreams and contemplates
      a carefree trip to the big city from the solace of a house hidden
Back in the woods.

The old writer hides
      hurts and disappointments behind the halo of a smile.
Thanks God daily,
      marvels at how He healed, restored, made whole, and
Saved a soul.

The old writer feasts
      on family phrases, same old story fellowship, friends and faith.
Understands transparency,
      insists on integrity and boldly writes past fear
To freedom.

My Brother's Story as I Believe He Would Write It

Daddy worked us children like slaves.
Our sister was the house servant.
She couldn't work in the fields much
Her being "sensitive" to the heat and all.
It's a family story now that everybody knows
To tell it right, you dramatically slap your forehead
With the back of your hand,
While faking a faint and sighing ohh...
She was told to go to the house before she got too hot.
We were told to get to work before he got a limb.
It just didn't seem fair.
She was allowed to stay in the house and cook.
She even got to use the fan.
We didn't like her much.
She's not directly tied to that most painful   memory.
It would have happened differently had she been involved.
It was hot that day.
It's always hot in Mississippi
When you work in the field,
Chopping the grass from around the peas or corn,
Careful not to cut down the plants.
Daddy worked in a contented rhythm;
The clean swipe of his hoe
Making the same perfect cut each time.
We worked in silence,
Cursing the ground with every stroke.
Still boys yet; soon to be made men before our time.
Doing our best to walk in shoes we were not big enough to fill.
Who knows what made him turn around?
"Ya'll give out?" he stopped and asked.
We looked at each other hopefully.

Jumping at the chance to go back to the house for a minute;
or even knock off for the day.
"Yeah! Yeah, we give out!"
We answered excitedly,
Nodding our head in unison.
Daddy removed his cap and wiped his sweat.
He squinted toward the sky,
He shook his head in his own wisdom.
He looked at us briefly,
Looked ahead pointedly.
"Don't give up," he said.
And kept right on working.
We looked at each other.
We wondered if adulthood
Could bring the sweetness of revenge.
We wondered if it could
Replace the reverent respect
of Southern reared childhood .
Finally, we squinted toward the sky,
Shook our heads in our own pity, and kept right on working…

Sugar Cane

    I remember taking thousands of stalks of cane and bringing back hundreds of cans of syrup.
    My mama remembered Jasper County, and somebody at Mr. So n So's house, pushing stalks of canes through the press.
    I remember watching a mule work but not how we got to the sorghum-filled buckets.
    My mama remembered a contraption was attached to a long pole, waiting for hours.

Around the Bend in Bean Station

Haziness of the fog
Above the water
Rises like steam
From my coffee cup.

Perfect peaks.
Nature's painted canvas
Whets my appetite
For a drink of beauty

Snow Days

Anticipation builds as
Children watch the sky.
Adults continue to work
Meteorologist are amazed
At massive snow accumulations
Below the Mason Dixon line.
Road crews talk about
 Brine, shovels and snow blowers
Resourceful residents use
 Brooms, spatulas and throw rugs
 The storm should go around.
It slams right into us
God-created weather lasagna
Layered sleet, freezing rain, snow.

College

We didn't have caller ID in the dorm.
We didn't know who was calling
 Until we answered the phone.

We laughed, had fun, and said silly things.
We said "Student affairs, would you like to have one?
We said "Donna and Shelia's massage parlor."

We accidentally said that to Daddy once.
We never discussed his response.
We didn't say it anymore.

My Appalachian Heritage

I wasn't born here
I'm just at home here

I go home to Mississippi
I come home to Tennessee

Cross the Tennessee River
Home to the banks of Chickasawhay

Lush green valleys, Tennessee mountains
Red clay dirt, Mississippi roads

Fall, bright yellow golden leaves
...Orange and white school colors

Spanish moss, hoarfrost...

Mississippi....
Birthplace to me and my first born
Tennessee...
The place my husband and baby call home

Mississippi flatlands and Tennessee mountains

Southeast Mississippi
Upper East Tennessee

I wasn't born here
I'm just at home here

I've lived, loved and lost here

I go home to Mississippi
I come home to Tennessee

Church Music

In Mississippi, they called it shouting
Commencing not with their voices
But with their feet as the music played.
"Pickin' 'em up and puttin' em down" for the Lord.

Even heavy ladies were light on their feet
On the old wood floor.
Their spiked high heels effortlessly
Stepping in staccato rhythm to the beat of the Spirit.
Making floorboards creak with each rhythm-ed step
But the boards held up for years.

The sound of those shouting feet
Sang a rhythm no voice could imitate or match.
When there was no piano,
 drums and tambourines kept time
Along with an old electric guitar…

There was something familiar in the rhythm for each song.

Men who seldom darken the door of the church
Stood outside the windows
Looking in and watching the ladies dance……

Lisa's Notes in the Sanctuary

Pause for Breath
A soft easy sound builds
Into an anointed crescendo
A full sonic explosion from her core;
Spurred on by an unbridled range
Crooning soft, low moans
Caress our ears and
Lull us to a quiet place
Notes held long, loud and strong
Sink into our skin and saturate our spirits
Living lyrics of *Amazing Grace*
Force melodies to take flight
Captured, floating past each pew
Resonating, reverberating off the walls
Filling our hearts with music
Compelling us to invoke the power
Of the notes as they fill the room

Aunt Pearlie and the Cartwrights

She will always be Aint Purl E to me
Linked forever to a Bonanza memory
She watched that show like a heavyweight fight.
To see her coach a brawl was quite a sight.
"Get wit 'em Little Joe! Watch out Adam!" she'd say
"Hoss better come quick before they get away."

"Where's Pa when you need him?"
"Them boys can use some help!"

Aint Purl E fought the battle with them
No matter how bad she felt.
She'd sit up on the couch
And we'd think, "Oh, boy, here she goes."
Those puny little arms swung out
As if she was really landing blows.

She watched with the same animation.
She always seemed surprised
To see us watching her when it was all over
With so much laughter in our eyes...

Driving Lessons

Sometime after the sight of
Naked wires sparking underneath the floorboards
Caused her to jump from a moving car, my great
Aunt Pearlie asked Uncle Duck to "learn" her how to drive.
It didn't go well.
With a white-knuckle grip on the wheel
She felt herself losing control of the car,
She was hollering, "Whoa! Whoa! Whoa!"
And Uncle Duck…
With his own wide-eyed, white knuckle grip,
Afraid she'd hit the house
Was hollering, "You ain't driving the mule, Aunt Pearlie!"
"Hit the brakes!"

Green Grass

When the grass is green
The world is doable
Everything and everybody
Copacetic or at least suitable
When the grass withers
Unattended hearts change
Neglected weeds grow
The garden's rearranged
Some try to cope
Others fix and mend
If nothing happens
Move to greener grass
And try again

Colloquial slang

The South...

Coke is any carbonated beverage
Slow is relative
Relative is kin
I got kin I ain't seen since Moby Dick was a minnow
In a mason jar.

The North...

Cokes are called pops
Pops are fathers
Fathers have kin everywhere
The kinfolk up north ran away, ah, I mean "migrated" from the fields "down south"
To the factories "up Nawth"

In the south, sweet tea is a soft drink
In the north, it's only sweet on "Long Island."

How to Make a Crazy Quilt

According to the website, it has nothing to do with one's state of mind and everything
to do with a distinctive, freestyle approach.

According to the first Dear John letter, it had nothing to do with falling out of love and everything to do with a desire to love freely.

Crazy people, crazy world, crazy patterns, crazy quilters
Crazy quilters, crazy patterns, crazy worlds, crazy people

Quilters are powerless to resist the urge to embellish their quilts.
Lovers are powerless to resist the urge to embellish their love.

According to the website, once you master the basic techniques of crazy quilting, you might want to look at inspirational designs to get ideas for your next projects.

According to the second Dear John letter, once you master the basic techniques of loving, you will want to look for ways to get that "loving feeling" again and again.

Crazy people, crazy world, crazy patterns, crazy quilters
Crazy quilters, crazy patterns, crazy worlds, crazy people

When it's done right, most people don't see craziness in the patterns.
When it's done consistently, most people don't see craziness in love.

The Woman and the Writer

The woman sees a mess of fallen leaves on the ground.
The writer sees blankets of pink snow-like petals beneath an oriental cherry tree.

The woman recalls multiple conversations heard at the family reunion.
The writer remembers stories of charismatic chaos, family fellowship unfolding.

The woman feels a hand on her shoulder, drifts off to sleep.
The writer feels the sweet caress of strong sure hands that warm her heart as she listens to his.

The woman matures slowly, eventually finds the path of God-ordained destiny.
The writer grows a little more quickly, already knows she and the woman are one.

Classically speaking as a Writer and a Librarian

I feel like I should love the classics
I don't
I feel like I should at least be familiar with most of them
I'm not
There are scenes I like from certain classics
I remember
Huck and Tom painting the white picket fence
Mark Twain
The red chief's ransom is engrained in my literary memory
O'Henry
I am enamored with historic homes in my home state
Rowan Oaks
I bought a copy of Abasalom! Absalom!
William Faulkner
Told myself I would read it right away
I lied
I feel like I'll always admire the classics
From afar
Just keep telling myself that one day I will read them
I won't

stories I heard growing up that became my own

funny stories about family responsibilities
silly tricks brothers play on sisters
"in my mama's story…"
the oldest girl…
babysitting children, cooking breakfast
while still just a child.
"in my own story…"
the oldest girl tolerated baby sister, heating oatmeal
in the microwave for them both
comical stories about real life characters
easter dresses, speeches, and church mothers
"in my mama's story…"
sunday dinner served on the "grounds"
fried chicken, peas, cornbread, cakes and pies.
"in my own story…"
sunday dinner served by harried waiters and waitresses
"church folk" labeled the worst customers and tippers
sad stories about racial stereotypes
the reality of living in the deep south
"in my mama's story…"
A little white girl running out into the yard
yelling "mama, mama, here come some darkies!"
as my mama and others in her family walked past
mr. so n' so's house
on the way to work one day
they would walk on
they were used to such outburst in the sixties
"in my own story…"
an elderly white man
describing president reagan's audacity
to hug a black gal on a national tv

as he walked into the public library to find
this 18-year-old black gal working behind the circulation desk
he would stop mid-stride
he was not used to such changes in the eighties
"in both of our stories..."
redemptive reflection of a past some
might choose to forget
the elderly gentlemen probably didn't live to see
the election of the nation's first black president
the little girl, if she lived would have
an opportunity to vote for him

Rivers Continued...

James Weldon Johnson sat the Lord down by a deep, wide river.
Another lay in the depth of Langston Hughes' soul.
A great wide river formed in my mind
Where the Jordan and Ohio Rivers converged
And became Freedom;
The river we crossed and laid our burdens down by.

www.ingramcontent.com/pod-product-compliance
Lightning Source LLC
Chambersburg PA
CBHW052129110526
44592CB00013B/1807